A gift for:

From:

Illustrated by Juliette Clarke
Edited by Helen Exley

Published in 2019 by Helen Exley® LONDON in Great-Britain.

ACKNOWLEDGEMENTS:
The publishers are grateful for permission to reproduce copyright material. Whilst every effort has been made to trace copyright holders, we would be pleased to hear from any not here acknowledged. Printed in China.

ISBN 978-1-78485-239-9

12 11 10 9 8 7 6 5 4 3 2

JANUARY 1

Hope smiles from the threshold of the year to come, whispering that it will be happier.

ALFRED, LORD TENNYSON

If you love this book…
you will probably want to know how to find other Helen Exley® LONDON gifts like it. They're all listed on
www.helenexley.com

OTHER HELEN EXLEY BOOKS

Words to live by...365

365 HOPE! DREAM! LIVE!

365 Make Someone Smile Today!

BE HAPPY!

LIVE! LAUGH! LOVE!

365 Happy Days!

Helen Exley® LONDON
16 Chalk Hill, Watford, Hertfordshire, WD19 4BG, UK.
www.helenexley.com

JANUARY **2**

My great hope is to laugh as much as I cry;
to get my work done and try to love somebody
and to have the courage to accept the love in return.

MAYA ANGELOU

DECEMBER 31

But warm, eager, living life…
to learn, to desire to know,
to feel, to think, to act.
That is what I want.
And nothing else.
That is what I must try for.

KATHERINE MANSFIELD

JANUARY **3**

Every day is a birth day;
every moment of it is new to us;
we are born again,
renewed for fresh work
and endeavour.

ISAAC WATTS

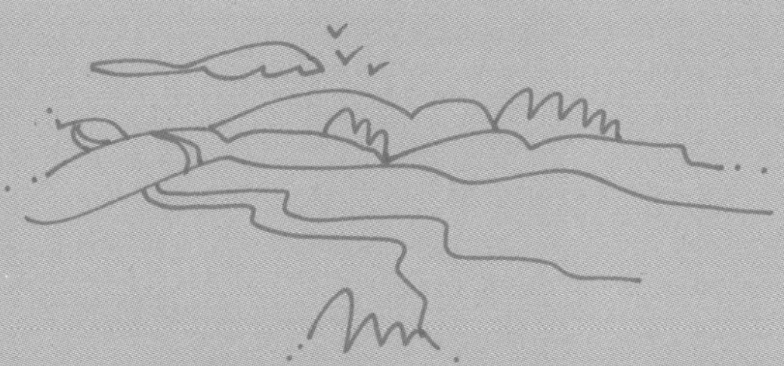

Each day the first day: Each day a life.

DAG HAMMARSKJÖLD

JANUARY 4

For new, and new, and ever-new,
The golden bud within the blue;
And every morning seems to say:
"There's something happy
on the way..."

HENRY VAN DYKE

BELIEVE YOU CAN
AND YOU CAN.
BELIEVE YOU WILL
AND YOU WILL.
SEE YOURSELF ACHIEVING,
AND YOU WILL ACHIEVE.

GARDNER HUNTING

Tomorrow is the most important
thing in life.
Comes into us at midnight very clean.
It's perfect when it arrives
and it puts itself in our hands.
It hopes we've learned something
from yesterday.

JOHN WAYNE

The natural flights
of the human mind
are not from pleasure
to pleasure, but
from hope to hope.

DR. SAMUEL JOHNSON

I'm a very positive thinker,
and I think that is what helps me
the most in difficult moments.

ROGER FEDERER

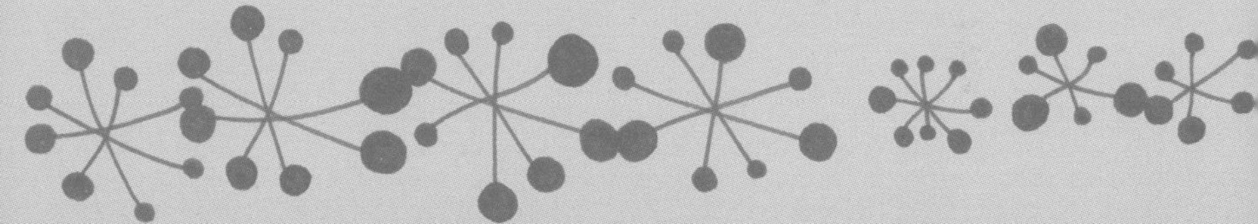

You may have a fresh start
any moment you choose.

MARY PICKFORD

JANUARY 7

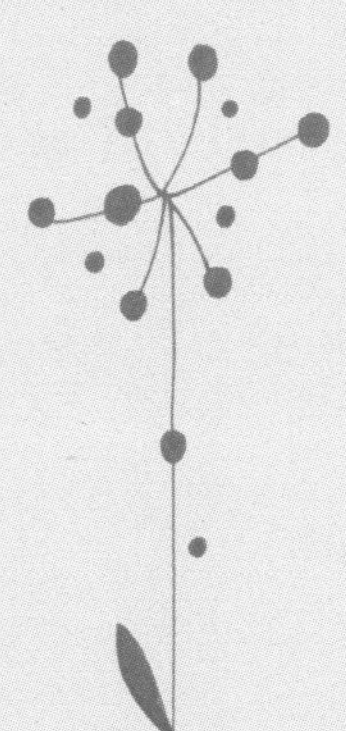

There is not a short life or a long life. There is only the life that you have, and the life you have is the life you are given, the life you work with. It has its own shape, describes its own arc, and is perfect.

GREEK PROVERB

DECEMBER **26**

Far beyond hope, the Spring is kind again,
lovely beyond the longing of my eyes.

MARGARET CROPPER

Isn't that the most fabulous thing about life?
Keep your mind open
and the universe
will just come in and give you
presents the entire time.

STEPHANIE BEACHAM

DECEMBER 25

We can complain because rose bushes have thorns, or rejoice because thorn bushes have roses.

ABRAHAM LINCOLN

JANUARY **9**

To me, every hour
of the day and night
is an unspeakably
perfect miracle.

WALT WHITMAN

Every day brings a chance
for you to draw in a breath,
kick off your shoes, and dance.

OPRAH WINFREY

JANUARY **10**

You can't use up
creativity.
The more you use,
the more you have.

MAYA ANGELOU

I always believed that if you put your energy into something, it happens.

SOPHIA LOREN

Everyone in this world has a gift.
Find it. Encourage it.
Astonish yourself.

ODILE DORMEUIL

You are never too old to set another goal
or to dream a new dream.

LES BROWN

JANUARY 12

Far away, there in the sunshine are my highest aspirations. I may not reach them, but I can look up and see their beauty, believe in them…

LOUISA MAY ALCOTT

The best song of your life
may be just around the corner.

KEITH RICHARDS

I love to wake up and meet the day.

GOLDIE HAWN

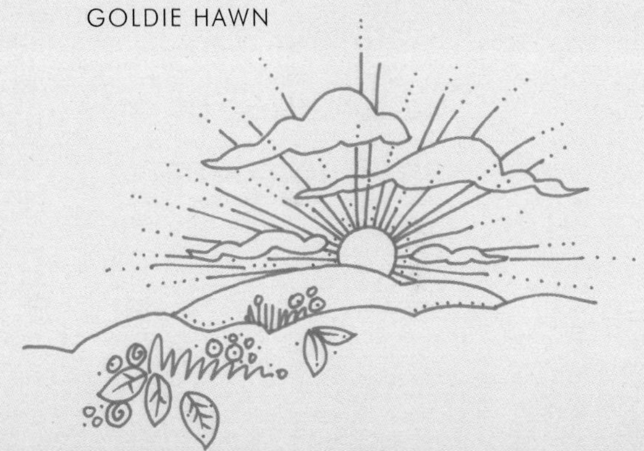

The love of life
is necessary
to the vigorous
prosecution of
any undertaking.

DR. SAMUEL JOHNSON

Yes is the most powerful word.
Yes is freeing and inspiring.
It means permission.
It means possibility. It means
you give yourself and others
the chance to dream.
Saying yes makes you feel good.

HOWARD BEHAR

Don't ever save anything
for a special occasion.
Being alive
is the special occasion.

AUTHOR UNKNOWN

Grant me the power to see
In every rose, eternity;
In every bud, the coming day;
In every snow, the promised May;
In every storm the legacy
Of rainbows
smiling down at me!

VIRGINIA WUERFEL

I once tried to count my blessings but had to give up – I couldn't remember if zillion came before trillion.

MATHILDE AND SÉBASTIEN FORESTIER

Always pack hope in your haversack.

PAM BROWN

Optimists may be wrong just as often as pessimists – but they have more fun.

FROM "THE FRIENDSHIP BOOK OF FRANCIS GAY"

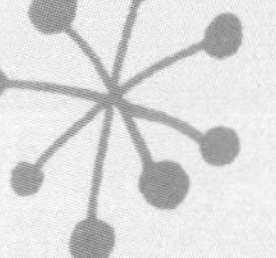

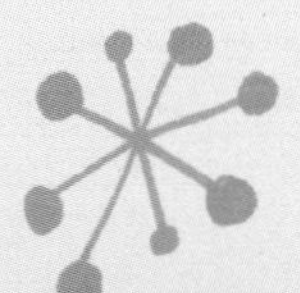

YOU ARE FREE TO RISE AS FAR AS YOUR DREAMS WILL TAKE YOU.

GERALDINE FERRARO

There is no dress rehearsal for life –
this is a live show.
So get out there and give it your
very best performance.

STUART & LINDA MACFARLANE

...there's the real danger of overlooking
a very important day... today.
For this is the place and the time for living.
Let us live each day abundantly
and beautifully while it is here.

ESTHER BALDWIN YORK

To improve the golden moment
of opportunity, and catch
the good that is within our reach,
is the great art of life.

DR. SAMUEL JOHNSON

JANUARY **19**

Look to this day! Look to this day!
For it is life, the very life of life.
In its brief course lie all the varieties
and realities of your existence:
the bliss of growth, the glory of
action, the splendour of beauty.

SANSKRIT

Nothing great was ever achieved
without enthusiasm. The way of life is wonderful;
it is by abandonment.

RALPH WALDO EMERSON

We should be blessed if we lived in the present always, and took advantage of every accident that befell us, like the grass which confesses the influence of the slightest dew that falls on it; and did not spend our time in atoning for the neglect of past opportunities... We loiter in winter while it is already spring.

HENRY DAVID THOREAU

TURN YOUR FACE TO THE SUN
AND THE SHADOWS FALL BEHIND YOU.

MAORI PROVERB

Keep your face to the sunshine
and you cannot see the shadow.

HELEN KELLER (BORN BOTH DEAF AND BLIND)

All people who have achieved great things have been dreamers.

ORISON SWETT MARDEN

Life presents innumerable opportunities for us to make choices. Life's literally full of choices. Choose love. Choose life. Choose hope. Don't give up on the very things that matter most. Trust yourself, we all have the strength, courage and power within us to make the right choices.

DALTON EXLEY

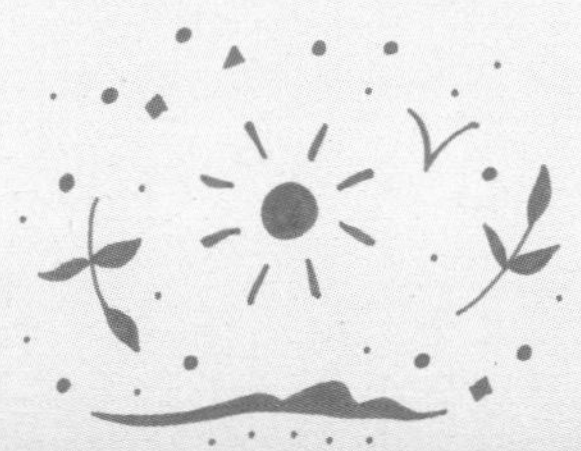

There are always flowers
for those who want to see them.

HENRI MATISSE

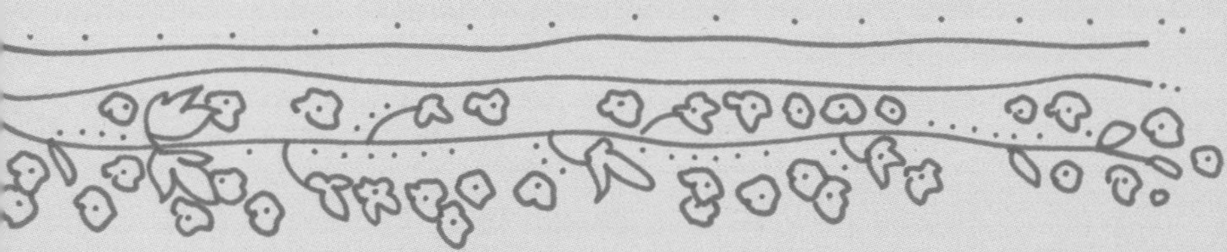

O Wonderful, wonderful,
and most wonderful
wonderful, and yet again wonderful,
and after that
out of all whooping!

WILLIAM SHAKESPEARE

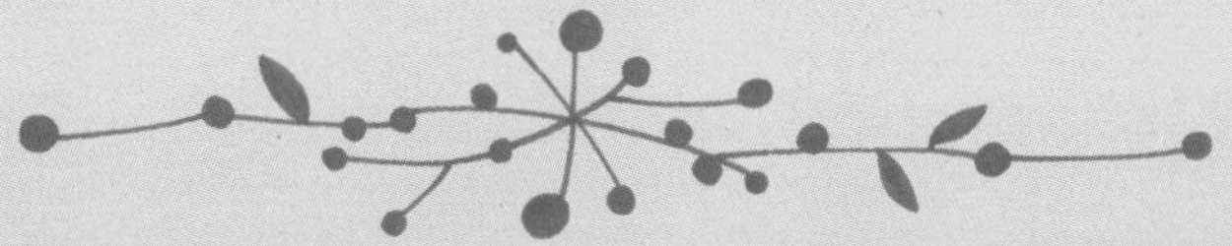

Life is short and in the brief time
we are here we should be the best,
the boldest and the brightest
we can be.

SHAUN MCILWRATH

JANUARY **24**

I am where I am because I believe in all possibilities.

WHOOPI GOLDBERG

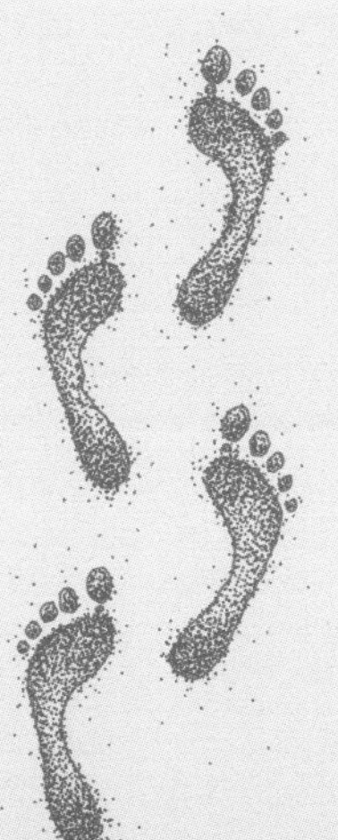

Hope is an adventure,
a going forward,
a confident search
for a rewarding life.

KARL MENNINGER

Be positive. Have only positivity going through your body. Be the best. Being the best starts by acting like U R the best. Believing U R the best. Becoming the best. Believe. Become.

SERENA WILLIAMS

Today is your day –
the day when you can
change your life.

STUART & LINDA MACFARLANE

JANUARY **26**

Increase your happy times, letting yourself go; follow your desire and best advantage. And "do your thing" while you are still on this earth, according to the command of your heart.

AFRICAN PROVERB

This is the best day
the world has ever seen.
Tomorrow will be better.

R. A. CAMPBELL

The human body experiences a powerful gravitational pull in the direction of hope. That is why the patient's hopes are the physician's secret weapon. They are hidden ingredients in any prescription.

NORMAN COUSINS

Write it on your heart that every day is the best day of the year.

RALPH WALDO EMERSON

Stay positive.

Be happy.

Live free.

AUTHOR UNKNOWN

DECEMBER **5**

STRETCH OUT YOUR HAND AND TAKE THE WORLD'S WIDE GIFT OF JOY AND BEAUTY.

CORINNE ROOSEVELT ROBINSON

JANUARY **29**

...cheerfulness keeps up
a kind of daylight
in the mind,
and fills it with a steady
and perpetual serenity.

JOSEPH ADDISON

The longer the island of knowledge,
the longer the shoreline of wonder.

RALPH W. SOCKMAN

When we really love and accept
and approve of ourselves
exactly as we are,
then everything in life works.
It's as if little miracles
are everywhere.

LOUISE L. HAY

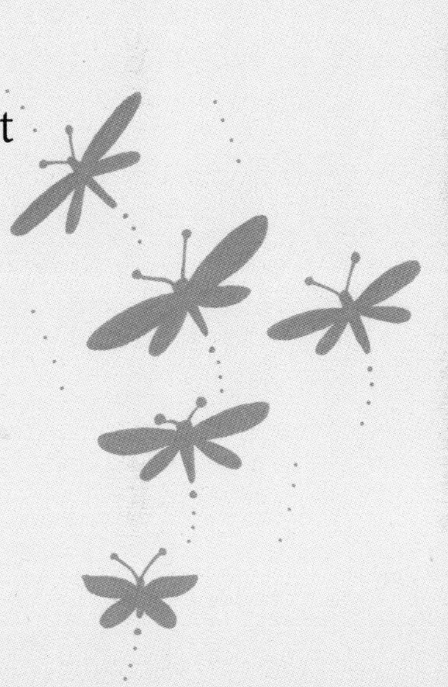

Be glad of life because it gives you the chance to love, to work, to play, and to look up at the stars.

HENRY VAN DYKE

Every new day is a new opportunity.
Each new day is a new chance to shine.

STUART & LINDA MACFARLANE

My advice to you is not to inquire why or whither, but just enjoy your ice cream while it's on your plate – that's my philosophy.

THORNTON WILDER

FEBRUARY **1**

I would be true, for there are those who trust me;
I would be pure, for there are those who care;
I would be strong, for there is much to suffer;
I would be brave, for there is much to dare.
I would be friend of all – the foe, the friendless;
I would be giving and forget the gift;
I would be humble, for I know my weakness;
I would look up – and laugh – and love – and lift.

HOWARD ARNOLD WALTER

DECEMBER 1

When your house has quite disappeared, you mustn't complain. You still have all that snow to do with what you like.

FROM "EEYORE'S GLOOMY LITTLE INSTRUCTION BOOK"

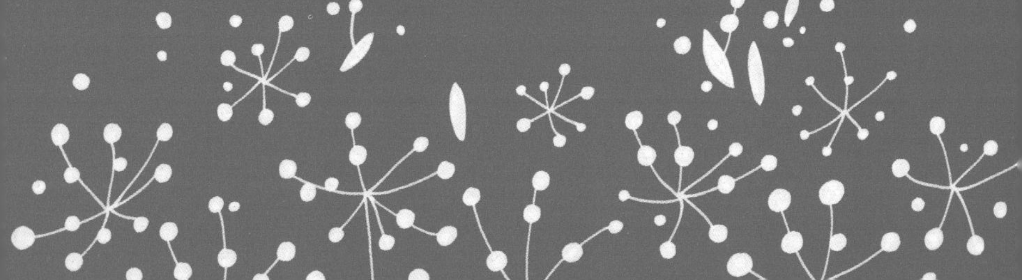

FEBRUARY 2

Watch when you're being negative about yourself,
it can have a worse effect than you think.
The same applies for how you deal with others.
Try to be positive wherever you can be in everything
you do and say.
It's a key ingredient for and a magnet of success.

DALTON EXLEY

There is so much in the world for us all if we only have the eyes to see it, and the heart to love it, and the hand to gather it to ourselves…

LUCY MAUD MONTGOMERY

Set your sights high, the higher the better.

Expect the most wonderful things to happen,

not in the future but right now.

Realize that nothing is too good.

Allow absolutely nothing to hamper you

or hold you up in any way.

EILEEN CADDY

The light is there
ahead of you,
a mere speck shining
in the dark –
but growing brighter
as you journey on.

PAM BROWN

FEBRUARY 4

Five things to declare daily:

1. I am amazing.
2. I can do anything.
3. Positivity is a choice.
4. I celebrate my individuality.
5. I am prepared to succeed.

AUTHOR UNKNOWN

The right time
is any time
that one is
still so lucky
as to have.
Live!

HENRY JAMES

You are the sum total of everything you've ever seen, heard, eaten, smelled, been told, forgot – it's all there. Everything influences each of us, and because of that I try to make sure that my experiences are positive.

MAYA ANGELOU

I want to live for ecstasy.
Small doses, moderate loves, all half-shades,
leave me cold. I like extravagance.
Letters which give the postman a stiff back
to carry, books which overflow from their covers,
sexuality which bursts the thermometers.

ANAÏS NIN

Happiness may pass –
but it will come again.
Certain as springtime
follows winter.
As sun comes after rain.

ODILE DORMEUIL

NEVER HAS
THE EARTH
BEEN SO LOVELY
NOR THE SUN
SO BRIGHT,
AS TODAY...

NIKINAPI

FEBRUARY 7

When you are joyful, when you say yes to life
and have fun and project positivity
all around you, you become a sun in the center
of every constellation,
and people want to be near you.

SHANNON L. ALDER

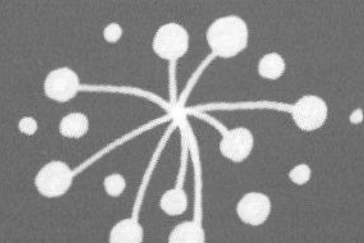

NOVEMBER **25**

Join the whole of creation of animate things
in a deep, heartfelt joy that you are alive;
that you see the sun, that you are in this glorious
earth which nature has made so beautiful
and which is yours to conquer and enjoy.

DR. WILLIAM OSLER

AS LONG AS
ONE KEEPS
SEARCHING,
THE ANSWERS
COME.

JOAN BAEZ

Keep on looking for the bright, bright skies;
Keep on hoping that the sun will rise;
Keep on singing when the whole world sighs,
And you'll get there in the morning.

HENRY HARRY THACKER BURLEIGH

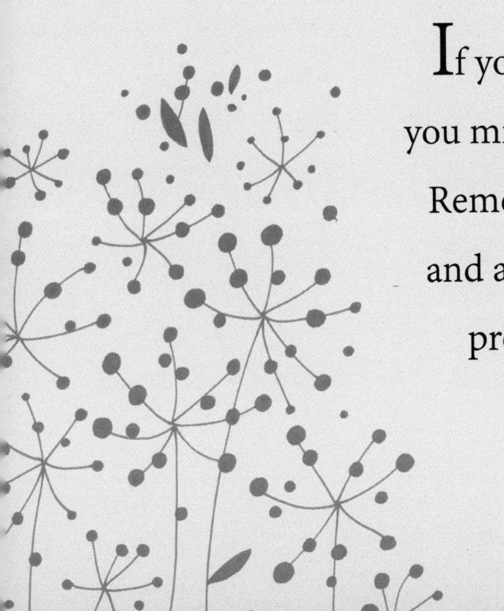

If you're going to think then you might as well think positive. Remember, positive thoughts and actions are seeds that will produce positive results.

AUTHOR UNKNOWN

NOVEMBER **23**

Some people see things
as they are and say why.
I dream things that never were
and say why not.

ROBERT F. KENNEDY JR.

Each second
you can be reborn.
Each second there can be
a new beginning.
It is choice,
it is your choice.

CLEARWATER

Forget pursuing happiness; pursue these other things and with luck happiness will come.

WILLIAM J. BENNETT

I have always felt that the moment when you first wake up in the morning is the most wonderful of the twenty-four hours. No matter how weary or dreary you may feel, you possess the certainty that... absolutely anything may happen...

MONICA BALDWIN

Life is available to anyone no matter what age.
All you have to do is grab it.

ART CARNEY

If we had keen vision of all that is ordinary
in human life, it would be like hearing
the grass grow or the squirrel's heart beat,
and we should die of that roar
which is the other side of silence.

GEORGE ELIOT (MARY ANN EVANS)

NOVEMBER **20**

We are here so short a while.
Savour the moment
as it passes. This is your
shining hour – all the glory
of the universe is yours.

PAM BROWN

...we are all waves of the same ocean. Some days the wave is big, some days it is small. Surf the wave you are given today and experience the rolling heights it offers. Validate yourself, your abilities, your gifts, your understandings. Validate your uniqueness...

BLACKWOLF (ROBERT JONES), OJIBWE, AND GINA JONES

NOVEMBER **19**

Nothing has to happen
for me to feel good!
I feel good because I'm alive!
Life is a gift,
and I revel in it.

ANTHONY ROBBINS

No matter what happens,
or how bad it seems today,
life does go on,
and it will be better tomorrow.

MAYA ANGELOU

Each step in Winter snow,
Each sparkle of Spring sunlight,
Each crunch of Autumn leaves,
Each sparkle of Summer sunlight,
Spell – REJOICE IN NOW!

STUART & LINDA MACFARLANE

Laughter is the joyous universal evergreen of life.

ABRAHAM LINCOLN

Positive thinking is powerful thinking.

GERMANY KENT

Spring –
the amazement
that is always
better than you
dared expect.

PAM BROWN

Don't think about what might go wrong,
think about what could go right.
Forget the mistake.
Remember the lesson.

AUTHOR UNKNOWN

Enthusiasm moves the world.

J. BALFOUR

Day and night I shall swim
in the sweetness-hope-river.

SRI CHINMOY

What helps me to go forward is that I stay receptive. I feel that anything can happen.

ANOUK AIMEE

NOVEMBER **14**

We all carry it within us:
supreme strength,
the fullness of wisdom,
unquenchable joy.
It is never thwarted,
and cannot
be destroyed.

HUSTON SMITH

I hope that I may always desire
more than I can accomplish.

MICHELANGELO

Every day is a renewal,
every morning
the daily miracle.
This joy you feel is life.

GERTRUDE STEIN

I dwell in possibility.

EMILY DICKINSON

If I had my life to live over...
I'd dare to make more mistakes next time.
I'd relax. I would limber up.
I would be sillier than I have been this trip.
I would take fewer things seriously.
I would take more chances.
I would take more trips.
I would perhaps have more actual troubles.
But I'd have fewer imaginary ones.

NADINE STAIR

You might think it takes an extraordinary person
to see diamonds in the mud,
but we can do the same if we decide to see
everything in the best possible light.

AUTHOR UNKNOWN

Those who wish to sing always find a song.

SWEDISH PROVERB

Everyone, every single human being in the world,
has something to give.
Something good.
Something wonderful.

PAMELA DUGDALE

And only when we are no longer afraid do we begin to live in every experience, painful or joyous; to live in gratitude for every moment, to live abundantly.

DOROTHY THOMPSON

A hope is stronger than a wish;
it is the feeling that the thing
we will for will happen.
It is the beginning of belief –
of faith.
And when we believe,
we know for certain
that anything can happen!

BOB PETERS

Always remember,
you have within you
the strength,
the patience,
and the passion
to reach for the stars
to change the world.

HARRIET TUBMAN

You are everything that is, your thoughts,
your life, your dreams come true.
You are everything you choose to be.
You are as unlimited as the endless universe.

SHAD HELMSTETTER

There is nothing worth achieving
that can't be achieved.
There is nothing worth doing
that can't be done.
No mountain too high,
no ocean too deep.

STUART & LINDA MACFARLANE

Dare to be strong and courageous.
That is the road. Venture anything.

SHERWOOD ANDERSON

Challenge is the core and mainspring of all human action. If there's an ocean, we cross it. If there's a disease, we cure it. If there's a wrong, we right it. If there's a record, we break it. And if there's a mountain, we climb it.

JAMES ULLMAN

We wake to gentle sunlight.
Stretch.
And smile
in the promise of the day.

ODILE DORMEUIL

Our way is not soft grass,
it's a mountain path with lots of rocks. But it goes
upwards, forward, toward the sun.

DR. RUTH WESTHEIMER

What were the odds of you ever
coming into existence?
A trillion never made it.
Treasure this extraordinary gift.
Delight in the wonders
chance has given you.

PAM BROWN

NOVEMBER **5**

At the end of the day give thanks
for the gift of life and make a vow that tomorrow
will be even better than today.

BRIAN CLYDE

FEBRUARY **28/29**

Accept surprises that upset your plans, shatter your dreams, give a completely different turn to your day and – who knows? – to your life.

DOM HELDER CAMARA

NOVEMBER 4

I can say there's no ordinary person, there's no ordinary day; every moment of life should be full. Every moment should be a fat moment.

ROSIE SWALE POPE

MARCH 1

I have found that if you love life,
life will love you back.

ARTHUR RUBINSTEIN

The more you praise
and celebrate your life,
the more there is
in life to celebrate.

OPRAH WINFREY

MARCH 2

Is there any symbol more redolent of regeneration than a seed, planted in rich compost, watered and warmed, to produce a new shoot of green in the spring, crowned by two perky, embryonic leaves? A tiny start, with the promise of plenty. It has taken me a long time to learn to look at those little leaves, and appreciate their significance, but I understand it now. And it has saved me from depression, even despair.

BARNEY BARDSLEY

Winter is on my head, but eternal spring is in my heart.

VICTOR HUGO

A single sunbeam
will drive away many shadows.

ST. FRANCIS OF ASSISI

Positive thinking will let you do everything better than negative thinking will.

ZIG ZIGLAR

MARCH **4**

I AVOID
LOOKING FORWARD
OR BACKWARD,
AND TRY
TO KEEP LOOKING
UPWARD.

CHARLOTTE BRONTË

I have become my own version of an optimist. If I can't make it through one door, I'll go through another door – or I'll make a door. Something terrific will come no matter how dark the present.

RABINDRANATH TAGORE

I don't want to get to the end of my life and find that I just lived the length of it. I want to have lived the width of it as well.

DIANE ACKERMAN

Don't cry
because
it's over.
Smile
because
it happened.

DR. SEUSS

If you think you can, you can.

MARY KAY ASH

Sunshine is delicious, rain is refreshing, wind braces us up, snow is exhilarating; there is really no such thing as bad weather, only different kinds of good weather.

JOHN RUSKIN

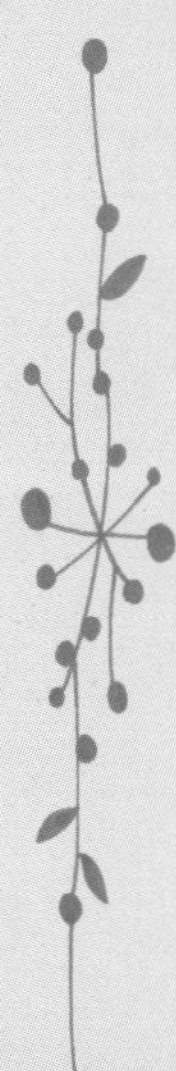

… Sometimes, when you feel alone,
It seems your heart will break in two...
But it won't.

And sometimes it seems
It's hardly worth carrying on...
But it is.

For sometimes, when the sun goes down,
It seems it will never rise again,
But it does.

FRANK BROWN

Each handicap is like a hurdle
in a steeplechase,
and when you ride up to it,
if you throw your heart over,
the horse will go along too.

LAURENCE BIXBY

MARCH 8

When you have goals
and a positive outlook on life,
you have something to aim for.

SIR RICHARD BRANSON

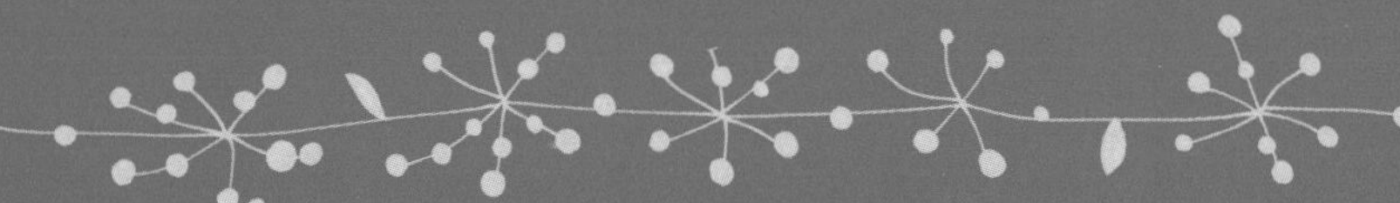

When life gives a hundred reasons to break down and cry, show life that you have a thousand reasons to smile and laugh. Stay Strong.

AUTHOR UNKNOWN

MARCH 9

Be glad.
Life is so rare a gift in this vast universe
that any price is worth the paying.
To have lived is to have been given
treasures beyond belief.
Treasures that can never be taken from us.
Stars and daisies, oceans and rain.
Love and kindness.
Even sorrow proclaims sentience,
proclaims wonder,
has a value beyond comprehension.

PAM BROWN

OCTOBER **26**

Laughing cheerfulness
throws sunlight
on all the paths of life.

JEAN PAUL RICHTER

Longings
innumerable
Longings
Exquisitely
Intense!

HASHIM AMEER ALI

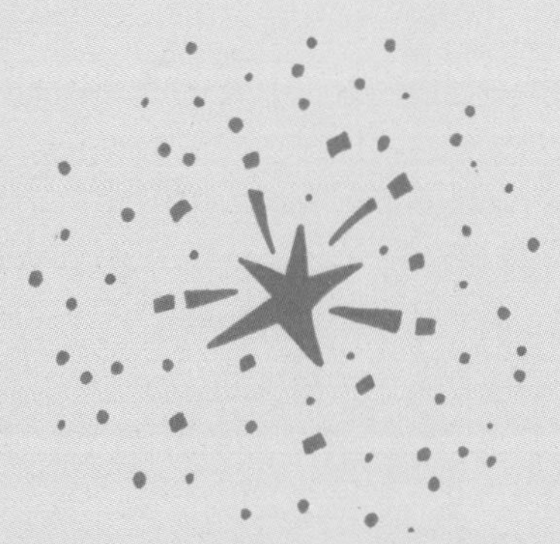

Once you choose hope, anything is possible.

CHRISTOPHER REEVE

MARCH **11**

In case you forgot to remind yourself this morning… Your butt is perfect. Your smile lights up the room. Your mind is insanely cool. You are way more than enough, and you are doing an amazing job at life.

AUTHOR UNKNOWN

OCTOBER **24**

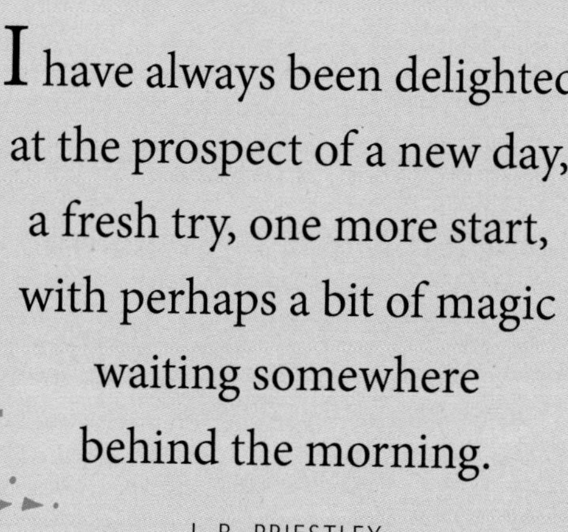

I have always been delighted
at the prospect of a new day,
a fresh try, one more start,
with perhaps a bit of magic
waiting somewhere
behind the morning.

J. B. PRIESTLEY

MARCH **12**

May you find happiness
everywhere you turn.
In love and friendship.
In music, theatre, art.
In mountains, oceans, deserts.
In woods and rivers.
In taste and scent and sound.

CHARLOTTE GRAY

OCTOBER **23**

Often people have a tragic story to tell – but rather than let adversity be a burden they let it become an inspiration to others in similar circumstances. These people who find hope – even in tragedy and, turn tragedy into hope.

STUART & LINDA MACFARLANE

Start where you are.
Use what you have.
Do what you can.

ARTHUR ASHE

We each hold within us a scrap of stardust.
Whatever dark engulfs us, nothing can put out its light.
Whatever foolishness distracts us it alone is constant.
It seeks the shining that exists in everything that lives.

PAM BROWN

I love people. I love my family, my children…
but inside myself is a place where I live
all alone and that's where you renew your springs
that never dry up.

PEARL S. BUCK

OCTOBER **21**

There isn't a train
I wouldn't take,
no matter
where it's going.

EDNA ST VINCENT MILLAY

MARCH **15**

I still find each day too short for all the thoughts
I want to think, all the walks I want to take,
all the books I want to read,
and all the friends I want to see.

JOHN BURROUGHS

Every second is of infinite value.

JOHANN WOLFGANG VON GOETHE

MARCH **16**

Successful people maintain a positive focus in life no matter what is going on around them. They stay focused on their past successes rather than their past failures, and on the next action steps they need to take to get them closer to the fulfilment of their goals rather than all the other distractions that life presents to them.

JACK CANFIELD

Be grateful
for this moment.
It is yours to mould
into any shape
of happiness
that pleases you.

BRIAN CLYDE

I believe in the sun, even when it is not shining.
I believe in love, even when I do not feel it.

AUTHOR UNKNOWN

OCTOBER **18**

You are surrounded by gifts
every living moment of every day.
Let yourself feel appreciation
for their presence
in your life
and take the time to
acknowledge their splendor.

LON G. NUNGESSER

MARCH **18**

I like living. I have sometimes been wildly, despairingly, acutely miserable, racked with sorrow, but through it all I still know quite certainly that just to be alive is a grand thing.

AGATHA CHRISTIE

Let go the sad times, hold on to the glad times, the picnics and parties and fun, the tingle and glow of a walk in the snow, the lazy days sprawled in the sun.

PAMELA DUGDALE

MARCH 19

A fluke.
Another wiggle and you would have never been.
Out of nothingness you came.
Out of star stuff.
Infinitely small changes
brought you to this.
To love.
To adventure.
To amazement.

PAM BROWN

OCTOBER **16**

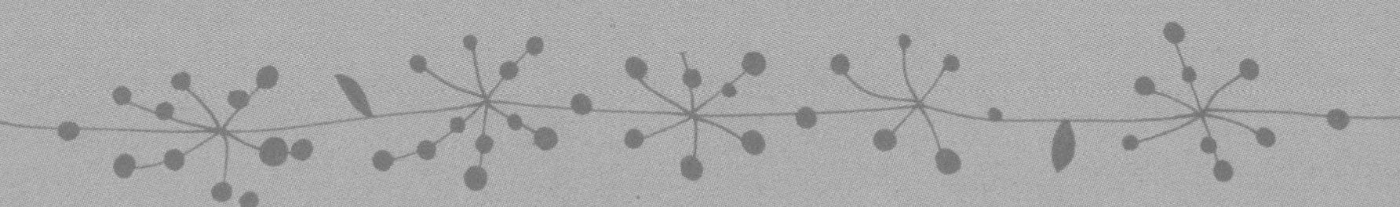

Every day it's nice to stop and say,
"Wait a minute! I am so lucky! This is great!"

KATE HUDSON

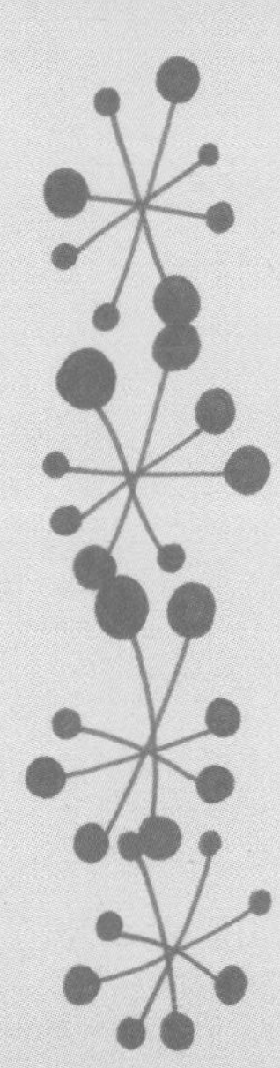

Shrug off the restraints that you have
allowed others to place upon you.
You are limitless.
There is nothing you cannot achieve.
There is no sadness in life
that cannot be reversed…

CLEARWATER

Life is a great big canvas;
throw all the paint on it you can.

DANNY KAYE

The warrior of life is a believer.
Because we believe in miracles,
miracles begin to happen.
Because we believe our
thoughts can change our life,
our life begins to change.

PAULO COELHO

The universe dreams a bigger
dream for you than you can
dream for yourself...
You've got to open yourself
to the dream the universe
has for you.

OPRAH WINFREY

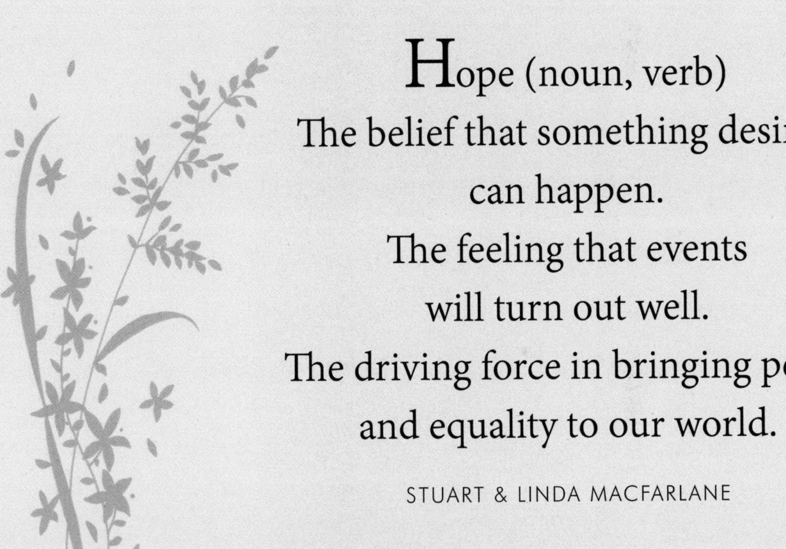

Hope (noun, verb)
The belief that something desired
can happen.
The feeling that events
will turn out well.
The driving force in bringing peace
and equality to our world.

STUART & LINDA MACFARLANE

The longer I live, the more apparent
it becomes to me that paradise
is not a goal at the end of the road,
but the road itself.

DOLLY PARTON

It's great to dare to dream.

BILL CULLEN

OCTOBER **12**

Each and every new day brings a fresh start, a new beginning, a new world full of opportunities and possibilities. It's a wonderful world.

STUART & LINDA MACFARLANE

You may not control all the events that happen to you, but you can decide not to be reduced by them. Try to be a rainbow in someone's cloud. Do not complain. Make every effort to change things you do not like. If you cannot make a change, change the way you have been thinking. You might find a new solution.

MAYA ANGELOU

OCTOBER **11**

Be thankful for this day.
The wonder, the tranquillity
and the laughter.
The happiness it has brought
into your life.
May it last forever.

BRIAN CLYDE

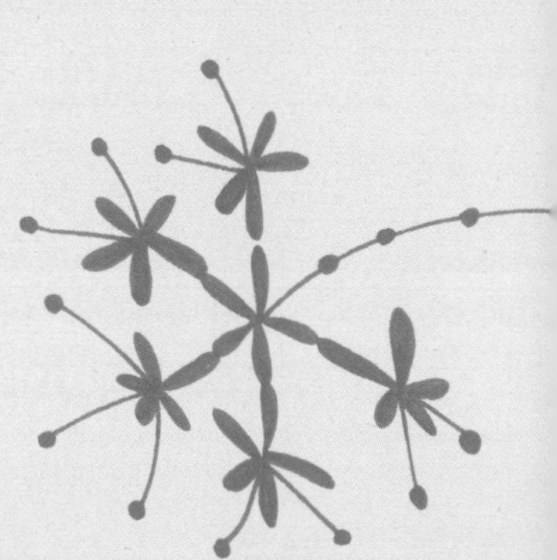

MARCH 25

He who binds to himself a Joy
Doth the wingèd life destroy;
But he who kisses the Joy as it flies
Lives in Eternity's sunrise.

WILLIAM BLAKE

OCTOBER **10**

Being positive is a happiness magnet. Good things and good people will be drawn to you. It'll surprise you, how good things will just happen to you and all around you.

DALTON EXLEY

MARCH 26

Each dip is followed by
a higher rise, and the overall pattern
is upward and onward, making true
the Latin motto
per ardua ad astra
(through endeavour to the stars).

A. C. GRAYLING

OCTOBER **9**

Behind the darkest cloud there is bright sunlight and following the dark sky of night there is always the promise of another dawn.

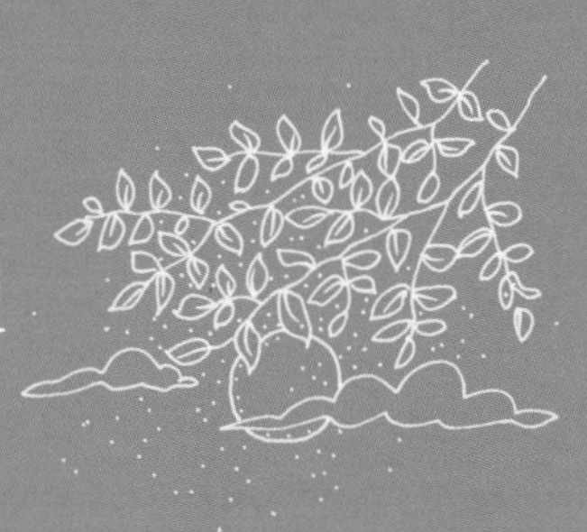

FROM "THE FRIENDSHIP BOOK OF FRANCIS GAY"

There are only two ways
to live your life.
One is as though nothing
is a miracle.
The other is as though
everything is a miracle.

ALBERT EINSTEIN

Don't waste your time
looking back for what you have lost.
Move on – for life
wasn't meant to be travelled
backwards.

AUTHOR UNKNOWN

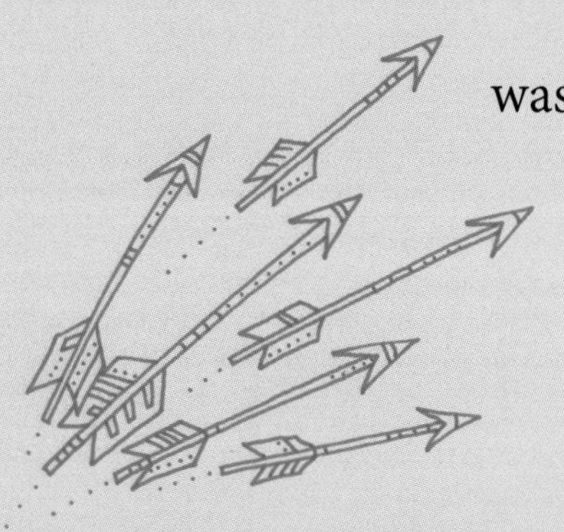

Plant for Spring.
Plant hope.

PAM BROWN

OCTOBER **7**

The difference between successful people and others is how long they spend time feeling sorry for themselves.

BARBARA CORCORAN

My heart is fixed firm and stable
in the belief that ultimately the sunshine
and the Summer, the flowers and the azure sky,
shall become as it were, interwoven into
our existence; we shall take from all their beauty
and enjoy their glory.

RICHARD JEFFERIES

When I feel so happy I jump to touch the sky,
When I feel so happy I climb a mountainside,
When I feel so happy I run around the world.

ANDREW MOSS, AGE 10

MARCH **30**

No more despondency.
Your life will become
The beauty of a rose,
The song of the dawn,
The dance of twilight.

SRI CHINMOY

OCTOBER **5**

In the depth of winter,
I finally learned
that within me there lay
an invincible summer.

ALBERT CAMUS

MARCH 31

What's the secret to making something happen in your life? Firstly, you have to want it enough. Then believe it can work. Then hold that vision and work out how it could happen, step by step, in your head, without the slightest doubt creeping in. Then, and here's the magic ingredient: just do it!

DALTON EXLEY

You will do foolish things but do them with enthusiasm.

SIDONIE GABRIELLE COLETTE

Remember this:
every time we laugh,
we take a kink
out of the chain of life.

JOSH BILLINGS

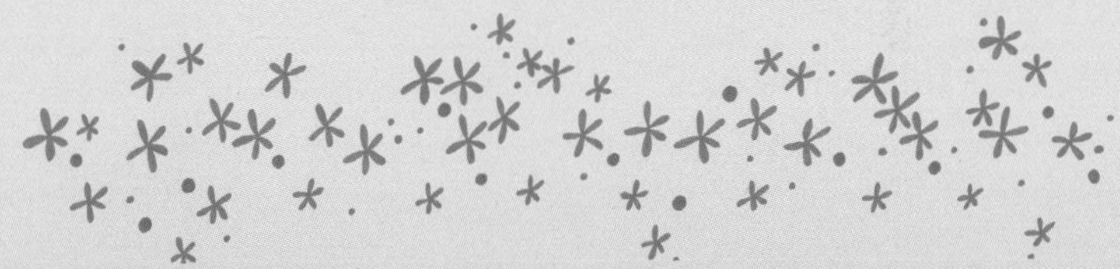

There is an excitement
in challenge,
in daring to fling open
doors– and if it all
fails it is not loss but
learning.

PAM BROWN

Don't look back
and ask why.
Look ahead
and demand
"Why not!"

AUTHOR UNKNOWN

OCTOBER **2**

BE VIGILANT;
GUARD YOUR MIND
AGAINST NEGATIVE
THOUGHTS.

GAUTAMA BUDDHA

Hope is something sweet, divine, and encouraging.

SRI CHINMOY

Never be afraid that your happiness will fade. Simply enjoy it while it is with you.

PAMELA DUGDALE

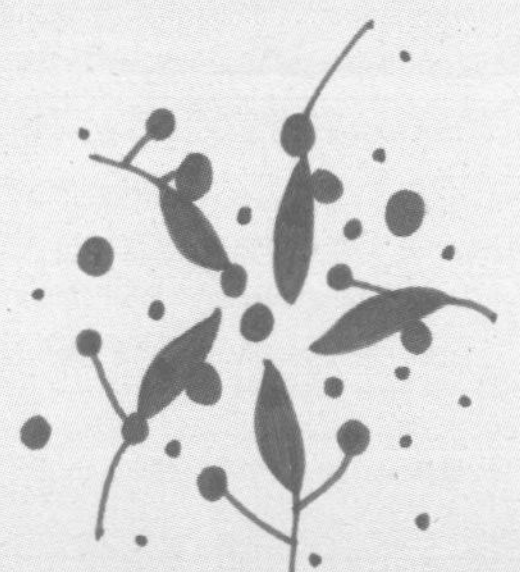

APRIL 4

More smiling,
less worrying.
More compassion,
less judgment.
More blessed,
less stressed.
More love,
less hate.

ROY T. BENNETT

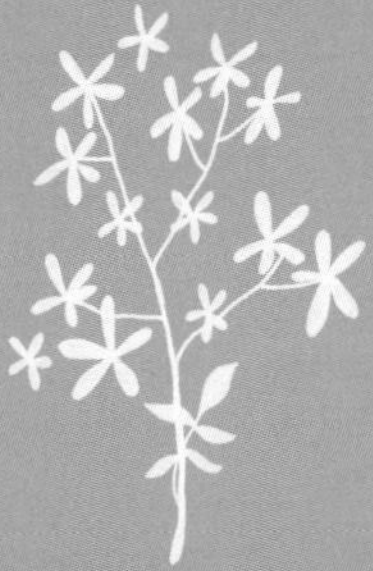

Always end the day
with a positive thought,
no matter how hard things were.
Tomorrow's a fresh opportunity
to make it better.

AUTHOR UNKNOWN

Faint not –
fight on!
Tomorrow
comes the song.

MALTBIE BABCOCK

Isn't it nice to think that tomorrow is a new day with no mistakes in it yet?

LUCY MAUD MONTGOMERY

May all your beginnings
be strong and true –
whether a plant, a tree, an idea,
A song, a book, a cabinet,
an engine. A family...

CHARLOTTE GRAY

What is alive, and open,
and active, is good.
All that makes for inertia,
lifelessness, dreariness,
is bad.

D. H. LAWRENCE

The washer's gone on the bathroom tap. When the milk's gone sour and you longed and longed for a cup of tea. When a windowed envelope wrecks your careful calculations. When the filling comes out of your tooth. When a cherished pot plant withers, leaf by leaf. When you mix the days and miss the concert. When you catch sight of your profile in a plate glass window. When you forget to turn on the last episode of a TV serial. When you don't win – anything.

Never mind.

Thank goodness that tomorrow really is another day.

PAM BROWN

So many reasons to be happy . . .

Family

Friends

Freedom

Love

Music

Sport

Laughter

You are ALIVE!

LINDA GIBSON

I am not a has-been. I'm a will be.

LAUREN BACALL

SEPTEMBER 26

If you are hopeful and determined, you will always find some measure of success. Winning the gold medal does not matter. You will have tried your best.

THE DALAI LAMA

This life is the gift
you have been given
– a world of wonders.
Enough to delight
a thousand,
thousand lives.
And it is yours.

PAMELA DUGDALE

If we did all the things we are capable of doing, we would literally astound ourselves.

THOMAS EDISON

You are wiser than you know,
cleverer than you know.
See what you can do and be amazed.

HANNAH C. KLEIN

You have your brush,
you have your colours,
you paint paradise,
then in you go.

NIKOS KAZANTZAKIS

THE BLUE
OF HEAVEN
IS LARGER
THAN
THE CLOUD.

ELIZABETH BARRETT BROWNING

Learn that there are two paths through life; one is a tortuous uphill struggle over rocky terrain squeezing through thorny briars, the other leads you across grassy dales with fragrant flowers past beautiful lochs with breathtaking mountains beyond. The paths are the same – attitude of mind makes them seem different.

STUART & LINDA MACFARLANE

Cheerfulness is like sunshine
to the day, or gentle renewing moisture
to parched herbs. The light of a cheerful face
diffuses itself, and communicates
the happy spirit that inspires it.

THOMAS CARLYLE

There is one thing I hope to have contributed to my children, by example and by talk: to make no conditions, to understand that life is a wonderful thing and to enjoy it, every day, to the full.

ARTHUR RUBINSTEIN

APRIL **13**

Life continually gives us opportunities
to grow and become.
For the most fragile flowers push
and grow out of the hardest rock.

BLACKWOLF (ROBERT JONES),
OJIBWE, AND GINA JONES

I want to see de children wake up
happy to de sunrise...
I want to see de loss of hope everywhere
replace wid de win of living.

GRACE NICHOLS

I shall no longer allow negative thoughts or feelings to drain me of my energy. Instead I shall focus on all the good that is in my life. I will think it, feel it and speak it. By doing so I will send out vibes of positive energy into the world and I shall be grateful for all the wonderful things it will attract into my life.

AUTHOR UNKNOWN

SEPTEMBER **20**

There's nothing that you can do that doesn't lead to something positive. I think it's all a part of life's journey. No matter what it is, it's good, it's part of the work you do here, it's part of the lessons learned.

DIANA ROSS

Attitude is a little thing that makes a big difference.

SIR WINSTON CHURCHILL

Always laugh
when you can.
It is cheap
medicine.

LORD BYRON

I move through my day-to-day life with a sense of appreciation and gratitude that comes from knowing how fortunate I truly am and how unearned all that I am thankful for really is. To have this perspective in my everyday consciousness is in itself a gift, for it leads to feeling "graced", or blessed, each time.

JEAN SHINODA BOLEN

To say yes, you have to sweat
and roll up your sleeves and plunge both
hands into life up to the elbows.

JEAN ANOUILH

A smile
is an investment,
An inner happy glow.
A mood-lifter,
A cheer-giver.

KATY CLARKE

SEPTEMBER **17**

I will arise and go now, and go to Innisfree,
And a small cabin build there, of clay and wattles made:
Nine bean-rows will I have there,
a hive for the honey-bee,
And live alone in the bee-loud glade.

WILLIAM BUTLER YEATS

The capacity for hope is the most significant fact of life. It provides human beings with a sense of destination and the energy to get started.

NORMAN COUSINS

Our lives are like the course of the sun.
At the darkest moment
there is the promise of daylight.

THE TIMES

There never was night that had no morn.

DINAH MULOCK CRAIK

I live by one principle: Enjoy life
with no conditions! People say,
"If I had your health, if I had your money,
oh, I would enjoy myself."
It is not true. I would be happy
if I were lying sick in a hospital bed.
It must come from the inside.

ARTHUR RUBINSTEIN

APRIL 20

Hold on to hope.
It seems so frail a thing
– but it will keep your head
above the water
while you find a foothold
and achieve the shore.
It's there just ahead.
So don't give in.
Firm ground and reassurance.
Waiting for you.

ODILE DORMEUIL

Today is the day,
A very special day,
Your day,
A day to cherish,
A day to enjoy,
A day to live.

MATHILDE AND SÉBASTIEN FORESTIER

Never look down to test the ground before taking your next step: only they who keep their eyes fixed on the far horizon will find the right road.

DAG HAMMARSKJÖLD

When you push a bulb deep into soft
wet soil, it is always a symbol of hope –
hope that nature will not fail;
hope that you will still be alive to see
the bulb burst out of the ground
and unfurl its delicate leaves,
opening the way for the flower.
It is about a future you can only hope for.

ROSIE BOYCOTT

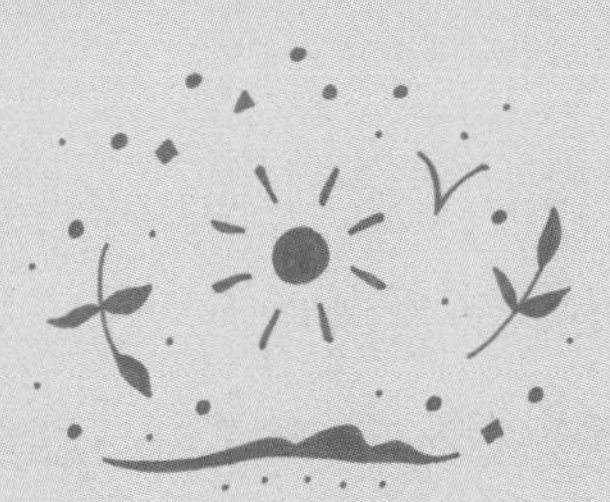

There is something good in all weathers. If it doesn't happen to be good for my work today, it's good for some other person's today, and will come around for me tomorrow.

CHARLES DICKENS

I have nothing to be thankful for...
Except the flowers that brighten up my life.
Except the rainbows that fill my skies with joy.
Except the mountains and hills and rivers
that make my walks a delight.
Except the love, friendship and companionship
that make every one of my days amazing!
I have nothing to be thankful for... Except!

STUART & LINDA MACFARLANE

A strong, positive self-image
is the best possible
preparation for success.

DR. JOYCE BROTHERS

MAKE VOYAGES!
ATTEMPT THEM!
THERE'S NOTHING ELSE...

TENNESSEE WILLIAMS

...you will discover your "alter ego". That is the person inside of you that is so committed to achieving your goal that you will become like the strongest of laser beams, capable of blowing away any obstacle that stands in your way.

PETER EBDON

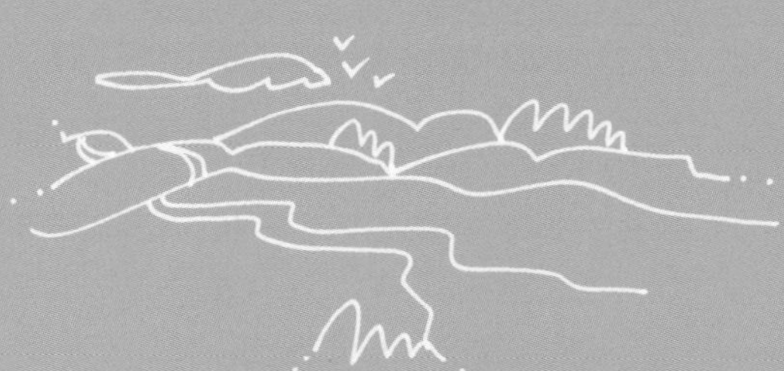

Hopeful as the break of day…

THOMAS BAILEY ALDRICH

I'm thankful for my struggle because without it, I wouldn't have stumbled across my strength.

ALEX ELLE

Your attitude is like a box of crayons
that color your picture gray,
and your picture will always be bleak.
Try adding some bright colors to
the picture by including humor,
and your picture begins to lighten up.

ALLEN KLEIN

Many an amazing spring
comes for you, in the seasons
and in your life –
– better than you ever dared hope.

DALTON EXLEY

If I were asked to give what I consider
the single most useful bit of advice for all humanity
it would be this: Expect trouble
as an inevitable part of life and when it comes,
hold your head high, look it squarely in the eye
and say, "I will be bigger than you.
You cannot defeat me."

ANN LANDERS

I live a day at a time.
Each day I look for a kernel of
excitement. In the morning, I say:
"What is my exciting thing for today?"
Then, I do the day.
Don't ask me about tomorrow.

BARBARA JORDAN

SEPTEMBER 7

No matter what you do in life,
always put your heart into it.
Live your life without regret.

AUTHOR UNKNOWN

We live in hope
and if that hope's
extinguished
– we find another.

PAM BROWN

THE GREATEST COURAGE IS TO GO ON HOPING WHEN ALL SEEMS LOST.

ODILE DORMEUIL

A smile creates sunshine
in the home…
fosters goodwill in business...
and is the best antidote
for trouble.

AUTHOR UNKNOWN

Always strive
to aim for the highest peak
of the goals in life you have set,
this way if you manage to reach
even half way toward a goal,
landing in the middle
is not such a bad place to end up.

VICTORIA ADDINO

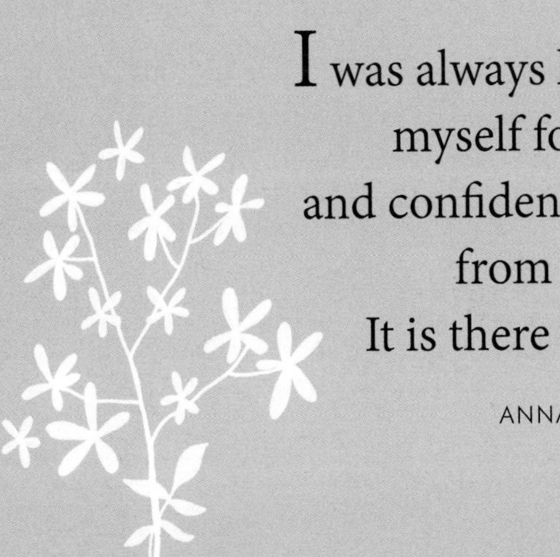

I was always looking outside
myself for strength
and confidence but it comes
from within.
It is there all the time.

ANNA FREUD

May you never
cease to search
and challenge.
May you always find
something to delight you.
May you always
have joy in living.

PAM BROWN

You yourself, as much as anyone in the entire universe, deserve your love and affection.

GAUTAMA BUDDHA

SEPTEMBER **3**

A feeble person can see the
farms that are fenced and tilled,
the houses that are built.
The strong person sees
the possible houses and farms.
His eye makes estates as fast
as the sun breeds clouds.

RALPH WALDO EMERSON

To be happy,
drop the words
"if only"
and substitute instead
the words "next time."

DR. SMILEY BLANTON

SEPTEMBER 2

I have smelt all the aromas there are in the fragrant kitchen they call Earth; and what we can enjoy in this life, I surely have enjoyed just like a lord!

HEINRICH HEINE

Success is a state of mind.
If you want success,
start thinking of yourself as a success.

DR. JOYCE BROTHERS

All our dreams
can come true –
if we have the courage
to pursue them.

WALT DISNEY

When you arise
in the morning,
think of what a privilege
it is to be alive,
to think, to enjoy,
to love...

MARCUS AURELIUS

No pessimist ever discovered
the secrets of the stars, or sailed to an uncharted land,
or opened a new heaven to the human spirit.

HELEN KELLER (BORN BOTH DEAF AND BLIND)

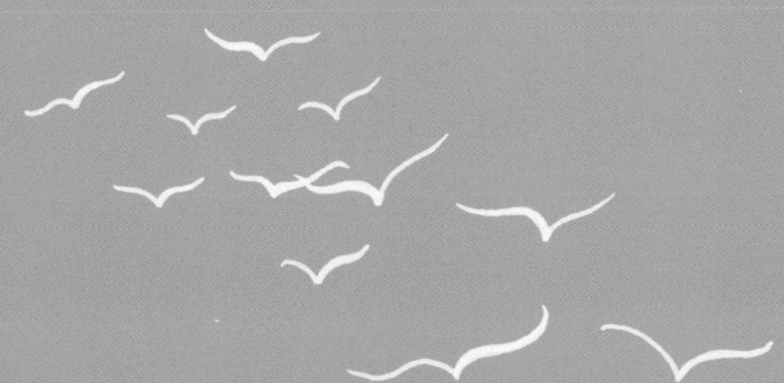

Today is a new beginning,
a chance to turn your failures into achievements
and your sorrows into so goods.

JOEL BROWN

Every problem has a gift for you in its hands.

RICHARD BACH

To have been alive is a gift beyond all others.
To have breathed air, heard kind voices.
To have reached out towards a smile
and be engulfed in love.
To have known birdsong, sea surge,
skies awash with stars.
One flower, one leaf, one rainbow.
That is enough.
All else is richness beyond belief.

PAM BROWN

Stop saying "If only"
and instead try saying "Next time".

DALTON EXLEY

If one is lucky, a single fantasy can transform a million realities.

MAYA ANGELOU

There are a thousand, thousand
reasons to live this life,
everyone of them sufficient.

MARILYNNE ROBINSON

HOPE HARD ENOUGH,
HOPE LONG ENOUGH
AND SOMETHING GOOD
WILL COME.

PAMELA DUGDALE

AUGUST **27**

All shall be well,
and all shall be well and all manner of things
shall be well.

JULIAN OF NORWICH

MAY 9

In this world, good is stronger than evil, love is stronger than hate, and somewhere, somehow, like a beautiful flower, this magnificence of the individual human soul survives through the worst of times. Through wars, through terrible mayhem, it plants itself, grows and flowers again and again. It walks on through the smoke of sorrow and holds up a blazing brush full of white paint.

ISABEL BEARMAN BUCHER

AUGUST **26**

The aim of life
is to live,
and to live means
to be aware,
joyously, drunkenly,
serenely,
divinely aware.

HENRY MILLER

MAY 10

Pessimism leads to weakness, optimism to power.

AUTHOR UNKNOWN

Learning to hope well is a small, quiet, subtle thing – but something that accumulates day by day into an unstoppable force.

STEPHEN BOWKETT

A positive attitude causes a chain reaction of positive thoughts, events and outcomes. It is a catalyst and it sparks extraordinary results.

WADE BOGGS

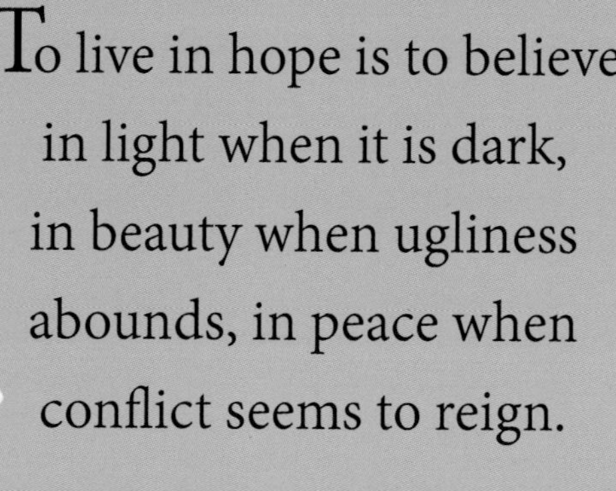

To live in hope is to believe
in light when it is dark,
in beauty when ugliness
abounds, in peace when
conflict seems to reign.

SUZANNE C. COLE

Close your eyes. You might try saying…
…something like this: "The sun is shining overhead.
The sky is blue and sparkling.
Nature is calm and in control of the world –
and I, as nature's child, am in tune with the Universe."

DALE CARNEGIE

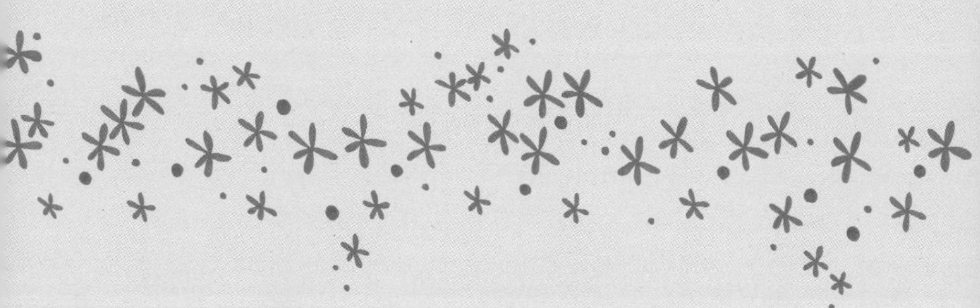

Today I live in the quiet,
joyous expectation of good.

ERNEST HOLMES

When your world's dark,
even a flicker of hope
can give life reason again.

DALTON EXLEY

It's often possible to turn negative situations into positive. Never feel a situation is all negative. There's a counterpart that is positive. Look for it, reach for it, utilize it – it will offset the negative.

BEAR HEART (MUSKOGEE)

MAY **14**

I have a sort of enthusiasm for life
and I don't ever want to lose it.
I like my life. I like who I am and what I do
and I'm quite at peace with myself.

JOAN COLLINS

What a fine lesson is conveyed to the mind,
to watch only for the smiles and neglect
the frowns of fate, to compose our lives of bright
and gentle moments, turning always
to the sunny side of things, and letting
the rest slip from our imaginations,
unheeded or forgotten.

WILLIAM HAZLITT

Three grand essentials
to happiness in this life are
something to do;
something to love;
and something to hope for.

JOSEPH ADDISON

Every word and every being
come knocking at your door,
bringing you their mystery.
If you are open to them, they
will flood you with their riches.

IRÉNÉE GUILANE DIOH

Opportunity dances with those who are already on the dance floor.

H. JACKSON BROWN JR.

AUGUST **19**

If there has been a secret to my success – a key ingredient or a personal philosophy – it is don't take no for an answer when you must hear yes.

JUNE JACKSON CHRISTMAS

Life is too marvellous, too valuable to waste.

LAMA SURYA DAS

Every day I wake up, I think,
what a blessing – I'm alive.
I don't care if it snows, it rains,
it thunderstorms – a heatwave.
I think, I'm here – this is terrific.

RICHARD HARRIS

To awaken each morning with a smile brightening my face; to greet the day with reverence for the opportunities it contains; to approach my work with a clean mind; to meet men and women with laughter on my lips and love in my heart; to be gentle, kind, and courteous through all the hours... This is how I desire to waste wisely my days.

THOMAS DEKKER

To love what you do and feel that it matters – how could anything be more fun?

KATHARINE GRAHAM

When one door is shut, another opens.

MIGUEL DE CERVANTES

AUGUST **16**

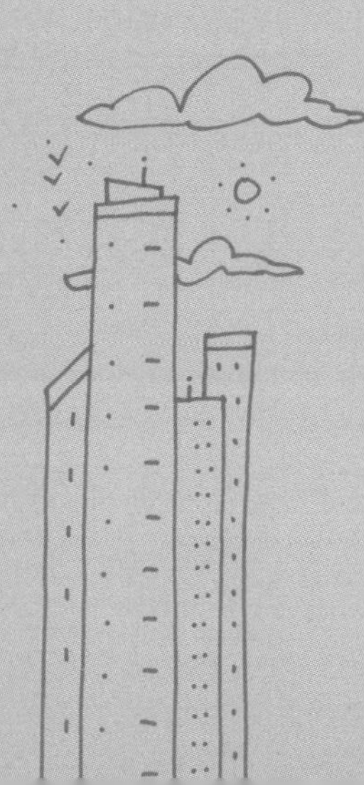

Like the weather, life
is essentially variable...
and a healthy person
believes in the validity
of his high hours
even when he is
having a low one.

HARRY EMERSON FOSDICK

Pessimists see the difficulty
in every opportunity but optimists
do better – they see the opportunity
in every difficulty.

AUTHOR UNKNOWN

The dark forest, destroyed
by summer fires,
will grow again.
New trees and wildflowers
will flourish in sunlight
that was never there before.

SUSAN SQUELLATI FLORENCE

MAY **21**

To fill the hour – that is happiness;
to fill the hour, and leave no crevice
for a repentance or an approval.

RALPH WALDO EMERSON

AUGUST **14**

This day is too dear,
with its hopes and
invitations,
to waste a moment
on yesterdays.

RALPH WALDO EMERSON

When the striving ceases,
there is life waiting as a gift.

SAUL BELLOW

It seems to me that we can never
give up longing and wishing
while we are thoroughly alive.
There are certain things
we feel to be beautiful and good,
and we must hunger after them.

GEORGE ELIOT (MARY ANN EVANS)

MAY 23

I think these difficult times have helped me to understand better than before how infinitely rich and beautiful life is in every way and that so many things that one goes around worrying about are of no importance whatsoever.

ISAK DINESEN

Anyone who masters
the grey everyday is a hero.

FYODOR MIKHAILOVICH DOSTOYEVSKY

In every day, there are 1,440 minutes. That means we have 1,440 daily opportunities to make a positive impact.

LES BROWN

Positivity, happiness, kindness and smiles are infectious! Start an outbreak!

DALTON EXLEY

No matter how negative my day turns out,
there is always one positive treasure to be found:
a beautiful sun-set, a baby's smile,
the soothing songs of the birds!
Nothing extraordinary, but how it helps us to see:
La vie en rose.

INGE BRANDT

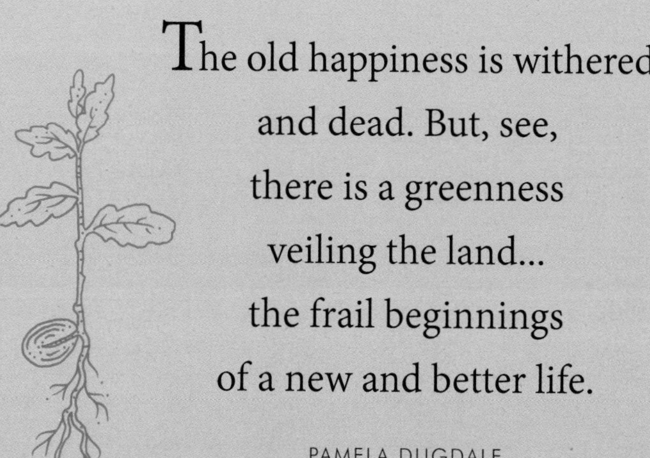

The old happiness is withered
and dead. But, see,
there is a greenness
veiling the land...
the frail beginnings
of a new and better life.

PAMELA DUGDALE

Simplicity, clarity, singleness:
these are the attributes
that give our lives power
and vividness and joy.

RICHARD HALLOWAY

Stay positive. The world
isn't going to get better
being negative about it.
There's two sides to life.
You choose which one you
want to live.

AUTHOR UNKNOWN

Beauty begins the moment you decide to be yourself.

COCO CHANEL

Though no one can go back
and make a brand-new start, anyone can
start now and make a brand new ending.

CARL BARD

When you finally allow yourself to trust joy
and embrace it,
you will find you dance with everything.

EMMANUEL

Every day must come to you as a new hope,
a new promise, a new aspiration.
If you think that tomorrow will be just another day
like all the days you have already seen,
you will make no progress. Every day
you have to energize yourself anew.
For it is only with newness that you can succeed
and transcend yourself.

SRI CHINMOY

Like a salmon swimming upstream, internal resistance challenges us to move against our fears and doubts. You can experience the same challenges with a positive focus or a negative focus. Find the positive and build on that. It will snowball into greater celebration.

BLACKWOLF (ROBERT JONES), OJIBWE, AND GINA JONES

Every smile makes you a day younger;
every sigh a day older.

CHINESE PROVERB

MAY **30**

Today is the first day of the rest of your life.

DALE CARNEGIE

What is the difference between
an obstacle and an opportunity?
Our attitude toward it.
Every opportunity has a difficulty,
and every difficulty has an
opportunity.

J. SIDLOW BAXTER

The secret of making something work in your life is, first of all, the deep desire to make it work: then the faith and belief that it can work: then to hold that clear definite vision in your consciousness and see it working out step by step, without one thought of doubt or disbelief.

EILEEN CADDY

One small positive thought in the morning can change the entire outcome of your day.

AUTHOR UNKNOWN

Good things happen to millions of people every day. Because so many have shared the same things does not make the joy less – it makes it more.

ROSIE SWALE POPE

AUGUST **3**

May you wake to sunlight,
stretch out your arms to embrace the day.

CHARLOTTE GRAY

Surviving means being born over and over.

ERICA JONG

Hope is a waking dream.

ARISTOTLE

I am an indestructible fortress,
I am an unassailable rock,
I am a precious jewel.

IRISH SAYING

AUGUST **1**

In the depths of winter
hope for spring.

PAM BROWN

JUNE 4

I will dare to do just what I do. Be just who I am. And dance whenever I want to.

SABRINA WARD HARRISON

JULY **31**

When the sun is shining
I can do anything;
no mountain is too high,
no trouble too difficult
to overcome.

WILMA RUDOLPH

JUNE 5

The sun rises on a new day
scattering yesterday into memories.
No matter what troubled you in the past,
the future is full of opportunities,
full of hope.

MATHILDE AND SÉBASTIEN FORESTIER

JULY **30**

We are all in the gutter,
but some of us
are looking at the stars.

OSCAR WILDE

JUNE **6**

…happiness comes through doors and windows we did not even know we opened.

FROM "THE FRIENDSHIP BOOK OF FRANCIS GAY"

I am still determined to be cheerful and to be happy, in whatever situation I may be; for I have also learnt, from experience, that the greater part of our happiness or misery depends on our dispositions, and not on our circumstances. We carry the seeds of the one or the other about with us in our minds wherever we go.

MARTHA WASHINGTON

Beauty is the flowers opening their faces.
Beauty is the larks gliding over dark blue clouds.
Beauty is the snowflakes drifting down on my head.
Beauty is the moonlight creeping up behind huge mountains.
Beauty is for plants growing higher, higher, and higher.

MANDY GIBSON, AGE 10

Raindrops –
Jewels that make up a rainbow.

LINDA GIBSON

You can, you know, just choose to be happy. Why not? Keep telling yourself you are and you will be. It's not really that hard to do. And, here's the thing, if you choose to be happy it makes others happier and so it goes around and around. On and on.

DALTON EXLEY

All theory is grey,
but the golden tree of life
grows green.

JOHANN WOLFGANG VON GOETHE

A child lives by little acts of courage.
Some jump into the pool, Some paddle.
Some clamber up a cliff.
Some dare to mount a little garden wall.
But all of them go out to meet the world
with all the courage they have got
and that is usually enough.

PAM BROWN

Those undescribed, ambrosial mornings
when a thousand birds were heard gently twittering
and ushering in the light, like the argument
to a new canto of an epic and heroic poem.
The serenity, the infinite promise of such a morning...

HENRY DAVID THOREAU

How wonderful it is that nobody need wait a single moment before starting to improve the world.

ANNE FRANK

I can… I can… I can… I did!

STUART & LINDA MACFARLANE

JUNE **11**

After the rain
the grass will shed its moisture,
the fog will lift from the trees,
a new light will brighten the sky
and play in the drops
that hang on all things.
Your heart will beat out
a new gladness,
– if you let it happen.

CHIEF DAN GEORGE, COAST SALISH

JULY **24**

Yesterday is but a dream.
And tomorrow is only a vision,
but today, well-lived, makes
every yesterday a dream of
happiness, and every tomorrow
a vision of hope. Look well,
therefore, to this day.

SANSKRIT

JUNE **12**

I thought I'd take style to its limit…
My philosophy is a belief in magic,
good luck, self-confidence and pride.

GRACE JONES

JULY **23**

If I were to wish for anything,
I should not wish for wealth
and power, but for the passionate
sense of the potential. For the eye
which, ever young and ardent,
sees the possible... what wine
is so sparkling, so fragrant,
so intoxicating, as possibility!

SØREN KIERKEGAARD

It's not about winning or losing,
it is about having the opportunity
to be in it, to really live your life,
to have purpose, and to enjoy it.

BILLIE JEAN KING

JULY 22

Let us rise up and be thankful,
for if we didn't learn
a lot today at least we learned a little,
and if we didn't learn a little,
at least we didn't get sick,
and if we got sick, at least we didn't die;
so let us all be thankful!

GAUTAMA BUDDHA

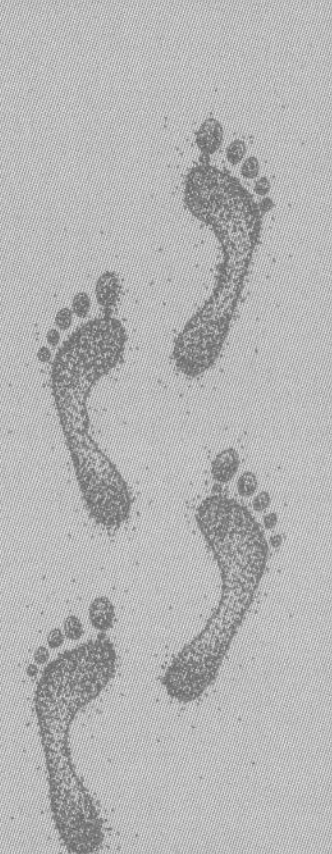

To look up and not down,
To look forward and not back,
To look out and not in, and
To lend a hand.

EDWARD EVERETT HALE

Somewhere, somehow,
in unexpected guise,
something good is waiting.

PAM BROWN

Never measure the height of a mountain,
until you have reached the top.
Then you will see how low it was.

DAG HAMMARSKJÖLD

JULY **20**

…it's not about running around the world, or indeed
going to the moon or climbing Mount Everest,
it is the adventure. Those adventures, they're fun,
but the real adventure is every single day
when you wake up, wiggle your toes and think
"Ooh a new day".
And you never know what will happen.

ROSIE SWALE POPE

The weather forecast says
"Rain! Rain! Rain!"
but your heart says
"Sun! Sun! Sun!"

STUART & LINDA MACFARLANE

To be able to look backwards
and say,
"This, this, has been the finest year
of my life," that is glorious!
But anticipation.
To be able to look ahead and say,
"The next year can and shall be better,"
that is more glorious!

FRANK LAUBACH

JUNE 17

Life is fun
Life is happiness
Life is gladness
Life is loving
Life is helping
Life is gentleness
Life is laughter
Oh, life is beautiful.

ALLISON HUDDART, AGE 10

JULY **18**

Walk on a rainbow trail;
walk on a trail of song.
And all about you
will be beauty.
There is a way out
of every dark mist,
over a rainbow trail.

NAVAJO SONG

Few things in the world are more powerful than a positive push. A smile. A word of optimism and hope. A "you can do it" when things are tough.

RICHARD M. DEVOS

The best is yet to be.

ROBERT BROWNING

I go everywhere without hesitation.
Hallelujah!

VIRGINIA BRINDIS DE SALAS

Hundreds of flowers in spring,
the moon in autumn, a cool breeze in summer,
and snow in winter.
If there is no vain cloud in your mind,
for you every day is a good day.

WU MEN

In the morning, how good it is to see
the brilliant light of the blessed summer day,
always brightest just after rain,
and to see how every tree and plant is full
of new life and abounding gladness;
and to feel one's own thankfulness of heart,
and that it is good to live...

GERTRUDE JEKYLL

There is always in February some one day,
at least, when one smells the yet distant,
but surely coming summer. Perhaps it is a warm,
mossy scent that greets one when passing along
the southern side of a hedge-bank; but the day
always comes, and with it the glad certainty
that summer is nearing and that the good things
promised will never fail.

GERTRUDE JEKYLL

May you always find
new paths,
new adventures,
new chapters of life,
new changes
to challenge you.

HELEN EXLEY

Every day the world gives you a special gift.
Twenty-four hours to do as you wish.
Celebrate the present that is life.
Use it in the most joyful, glorious ways.

MATHILDE AND SÉBASTIEN FORESTIER

DANCE, my heart;
O dance today with joy!

KABIR

Paradise is where I am.

VOLTAIRE

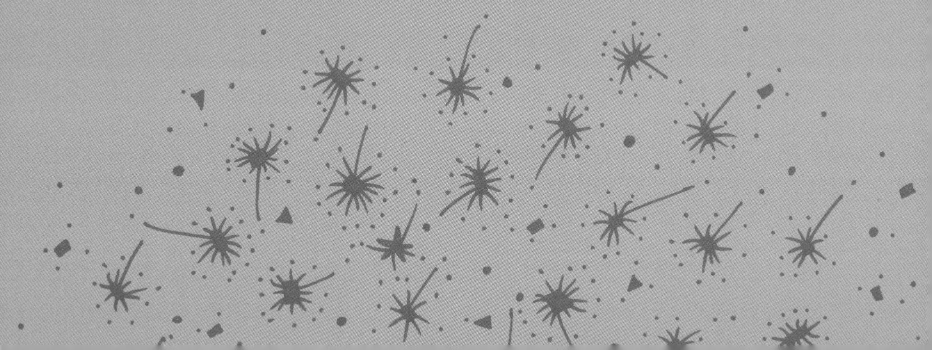

Love the moment. Flowers grow out of dark moments.
Therefore, each moment is vital.
It affects the whole. Life is a succession of such moments
and to live each, is to succeed.

CORITA KENT

JULY **12**

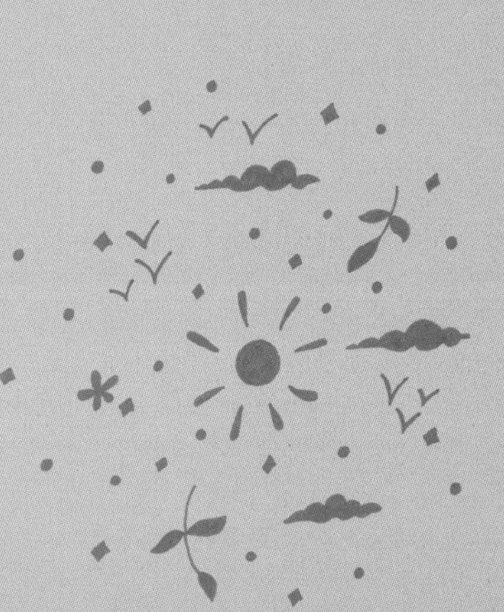

I wish you this day –
a special day,
full of hope,
fresh promise
and new beginnings.

DALTON EXLEY

Work hard for what you want because it won't come to you without a fight. You have to be strong and courageous and know that you can do anything you put your mind to. If somebody puts you down or criticizes you, just keep on believing in yourself and turn it into something positive.

LEAH LABELLE

Hope. You cannot see it
with your eyes and yet
it radiates from you,
filling those around you
with belief.

STUART & LINDA MACFARLANE

For myself I am an optimist – it does not seem to be much use to be anything else.

SIR WINSTON CHURCHILL

I don't think of all the misery,
but of the beauty that still remains.

ANNE FRANK

JUNE 26

It doesn't matter if you work
seventeen hours a day.
If you want to get there, you will,
because you are positive. You will achieve.
It's when you become negative
that you let yourself down.

VIRGINIA LOPALCO

A new life begins for us with every second.
Let us go forward joyously to meet it.
We must press on, whether we will or not,
and we shall walk better with our eyes before us
than with them ever cast behind.

JEROME K. JEROME

I am only one,
But still I am one.
I cannot do everything,
But still I can do something;
And because I cannot do everything
I will not refuse to do the something
that I can do.

EDWARD EVERETT HALE

My creed is this:

Happiness is the only good.

The place to be happy is here.

The time to be happy is now.

ROBERT GREEN INGERSOLL

JUNE **28**

Happiness, not in another place but this place...
not for another hour, but this hour.

WALT WHITMAN

JULY 7

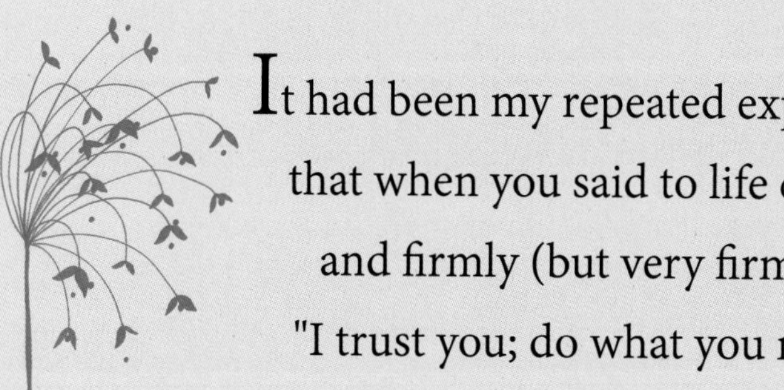

It had been my repeated experience that when you said to life calmly and firmly (but very firmly!), "I trust you; do what you must," life had an uncanny way of responding to your need.

OLGA ILYIN

If you ask me what I came into this life to do,
I will tell you: I came to live out loud.

EMILE ZOLA

You were made for enjoyment, and the world was filled with things which you will enjoy.

JOHN RUSKIN

Normal day, let me be aware of
the treasure you are. Let me learn from you,
love you, bless you before you depart.
Let me not pass you by in quest
of some rare and perfect tomorrow.
Let me hold you while I may...

MARY JEAN IRION

Then and there I invented this rule for myself to be applied to every decision I might have to make in the future. I would sort out all the arguments and see which belonged to fear and which to creativeness... I think it must be a rule something like this that makes jonquils and crocuses come pushing through the cold mud.

KATHARINE BUTLER HATHAWAY

The positive thinker
sees the invisible, feels the intangible,
and achieves the impossible.

SIR WINSTON CHURCHILL

Each new day
is an opportunity
to start all over again...
to clarify our vision.

JO PETTY

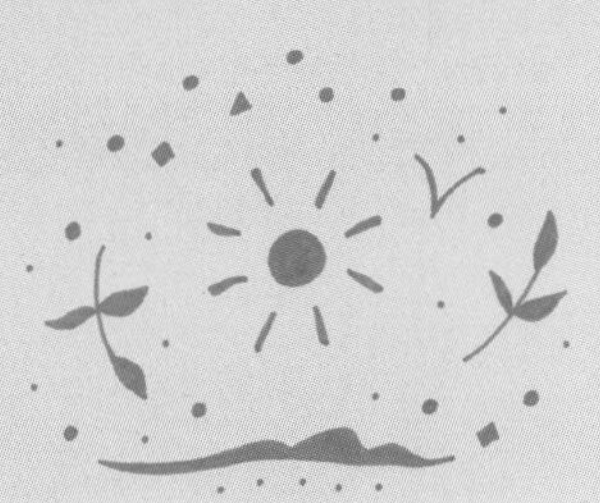

I WILL ALWAYS FIND A WAY

AND A WAY WILL ALWAYS FIND ME.

CHARLES F. GLASSMAN

It begins with the vision
to recognize when a job, a life stage,
a relationship, is over –
and let it go.
It involves a sense of the future,
a belief that every exit line
is an entry, that we are moving on,
rather than out.

ELLEN GOODMAN